# AT HOME

If where you live is full of trees, then your house might look like this. In the warm Philippines houses are open and cool.

But in Sweden, where the weather is cold, thick logs are used to hold the snow and ice at bay.

On the tiny islands of Lake Titicaca, some Peruvians build houses from the reeds that grow there.

In Malaysia houses are built over water. Houses on legs stand very high, all the better to keep your feet dry!

In the Philippines, too, on marshy ground, a whole village on stilts spreads all around.

If it is really wet, with water all around, a boat's the place to be.
This Vietnamese boat is home for this boy and his family.

This South African house is made of wood and woven branches, so it's quick to put up and easy to take down.

This other South African house is the same shape – and looks a bit like half an orange!

In cold Iceland, where there's not much sun, houses have many windows to let the light in.

In Siberia these reindeer farmers are always on the move – so their homes move with them. A simple tent is all they need.

In **Greenland** in winter, when snow is all around, homes can be made from ice blocks dug out from the ground.

A house made of ice can be surprisingly nice with a little fire inside to keep it cosy and warm. This igloo is in Canada.

A big, round yurt is the name for this Mongolian tent;
it has a stove in the middle for cooking the food.

In the middle of the Sahara Desert we find this Bedouin
tent. It has rugs all around to make it look pleasant.

In Cameroon, where trees are scarce, the houses are made of dried mud.

They use mud in Mali to build their homes too – houses that are like sandcastles, made out of earth.

In Ghana they paint patterns and pictures on the walls. These women are painting crocodiles on the walls of their homes.

A house is somewhere to feel safe and secure. In Mali these people live inside a cliff – safe from the outside world.

When the seasons change these Kazakh people in Mongolia move house – this season they're living in a house made of mud bricks.

Houses can move too, like this American caravan – it's made of shiny metal and is pulled by a car.

Is it a house or is it a work of art? With all these paintings this Egyptian house looks like an art gallery.

Walls covered in bright designs – it seems the Ndebele people in South Africa love their colourful homes.

In this Lebanese city there are houses upon houses, thousands of houses where people live.

In Japan the buildings reach for the sky,
giant-sized houses rise up from the ground.

In Greece it is hot and the houses are white. The light colour helps to keep the houses cool.

What a strange shape this Tunisian house is! It's actually a rock that has been hollowed out into stairs and rooms and balconies that stick out.

This beautiful building is painted white and blue.
In Bhutan this monastery is where monks live.